You Have A Date, Don't F It Up

CASSIE LEIGH

TITLES BY CASSIE LEIGH

DATING FOR MEN
Online Dating for Men: The Basics
Don't Be a Douchebag
You Have a Date, Don't F It Up
The How to Meet a Woman Collection

DATING FOR WOMEN
Online Dating for Women: The Basics
Online Dating is Hell

DOG-RELATED
Puppy Parenting Basics
Puppy Parenting in an Apartment
Dog Park Basics

COOKING-RELATED
You Can't Eat the Pretty

CONTENTS

INTRODUCTION

Well, it's that time again. Time to knock you upside the head about silly dating mistakes that might be costing you that chance at ever-lasting love and happiness. Or, if nothing else, another date.

This book is for those who've mastered (or think they have) the first step of dating—getting a woman to agree to go out with you—and are now trying to figure out how to get from "yes, I'll go out with you" to the actual date and from that first date to a second and from a second to a third.

Beyond that point any advice—other than be a nice person and listen to the woman you're dating and give her what she wants—starts to fall apart.

(This goes without saying, but you should also be getting what you want out of the relationship, too. And if you can't get enough of what you want while giving her enough of what she wants, it's not going to work.)

Anyway. Back to the point of this book.

While my other books have focused on online dating, this book should apply to any sort of dating. There are definitely differences between going on a first date with someone you've only met online versus going on a date with someone you've actually met in real life, but most of the principles we'll talk about apply to both.

As I've said in my other books, I can't speak for all women, I can only speak for myself. Why one particular date you went on didn't work will have to remain one of life's eternal mysteries. What I can do is give you some insights based on my own personal experiences and reactions.

And since I'm one of the pickiest, most judgmental people I know when it comes to dating—not that most men realize this, which is part of what you need to understand about women—if you can make it past my deal-breakers you should be golden with most women.

Can I guarantee that you'll be successful with *all* women after you read this book? No. And you shouldn't want that. Because some people just aren't compatible and it's fine to acknowledge that and move on to better prospects. (Even if she's really attractive.)

Hopefully after reading this book you'll be able to fix the basic mistakes a lot of men make that lose them that chance of dating someone wonderful for them. By the time you're done, you should be able to (a) make it to the actual date, (b) have a good enough time that there's a second one if you're interested and interesting to her, and (c) maybe even make it to the next date after that. Beyond that point, whether things continue forward or not will very much be a matter of you and the individual woman you're dating.

One last thing before we get started: As stated in my other books, I'm writing this book for men interested in dating women. If you're a man looking for men, some of what I say here is probably applicable, but a lot won't be. Same for a woman looking for men or women.

So, this book is for men wanting to date women and not doing as well as they'd like.

DOES THIS SOUND FAMILIAR?

You meet a woman you like. She's attractive and interesting and you guys seem to hit it off, so you ask her out. And she say yes. Congratulations! You have a date with a woman you'd like to see more of.

But…

When you try to call her, she doesn't answer. (Or you find out she gave you a fake number.)

Or if she does answer, she blows you off before you can talk.

Or when you try to make plans to get together, she's constantly busy.

Or she agrees to get together, but somewhere in between agreeing to get together and actually setting up firm plans, she bails on you. Maybe she says she's just too busy right now. Maybe she just stops responding.

Maybe you do make plans and she stands you up.

Or cuts out before the date has really begun.

Or you guys have what seems like a great first date and then…nothing. You never hear from her again.

I'll admit it. I'm guilty of all of the above except standing a guy up and cutting out early once a date starts.

(Those two I think are rude, so if I have firm plans with a guy I'll go on the date and suffer through it no matter how miserable. Or I'll be decent enough to cancel in advance.)

But all of the rest?

Yep. Done that. More than once.

Why? Why do women say they'll go out with you and then bail? (Men do this, too, by the way. This isn't isolated to women. But for this book we'll focus on women and why they do these things and how you can avoid having it happen to you as often as it may be happening now.)

What went wrong?

How did you go from a woman who seemed interested to radio silence?

Or, worse, a woman who actually met up with you and seemed to have a good time to a woman who never took your calls again?

Well, let's start at the beginning, shall we?

FIRST, DID SHE ACTUALLY AGREE TO GO OUT WITH YOU?

Ah, weren't expecting that were you? You figured that if you asked a woman for her number and she gave it to you that that actually meant something.

Nope. Doesn't mean a thing.

I am not proud of this, but, especially when I was younger, I would give my number to men who asked for it with no intent of ever speaking to them again. (Or, in the pre-cellphone days, I'd say I couldn't give out my number because my dad didn't like me to—which was actually true because I wasn't capable of giving a fake number and he had to screen the calls—and I would take men's numbers instead and then I'd never call.)

Why?

Why do women do this?

Honest answer: Because it's much easier than the alternative, which is to tell some perfectly nice guy that even though I barely know him I already know I'm not interested.

I mean, what am I supposed to say? "Um, you know, I'm really just not that into men with beards."

CASSIE LEIGH

Or, true example, "While it's great that you flunked out of community college five times and now work as a parking lot attendant that's just not the kind of guy I picture myself with."

Instead, I say sure, take the number and move on with my life without some ugly scene. Because I've learned through more than one unpleasant encounter that saying no results in one of two outcomes, both of which I don't want to deal with.

In the first scenario the guy asks, "Why not?"

This can either be a perfectly legitimate question asked by a nice, decent guy. Like, "Hey, I thought we were getting along, why wouldn't you want to see me again?"

Or it can be asked as a defensive, "What the hell? I thought we were cool" sort of question.

Whichever tone the guy takes, it's not fun to have to explain to someone that they just didn't spark things enough for you to want to keep it going. And sometimes the reason a guy isn't interesting is something you don't want to share. You know like, "I can't stop staring at your unibrow and it really just bugs the shit out of me."

(At which point the guy says, "I could shave it, it's not that big a deal" but I'm thinking, "But you're still the type of guy who didn't even realize that having a bushy unibrow would be a turn-off to a lot of women. And what else do I not see right now that's going to be like that? And, seriously, you're just willing to change on a dime for a woman you just met so she'll go out with you? Have some pride, man. Stand up for your beliefs and find a woman who loves her a sexy unibrow-wearing crazy man.")

Anyway. It's not a conversation anyone wants to have. I don't live to hurt others' feelings and, believe it or not, screening a guy's call is a lot less painful than any in-person critique I could give. By giving him my number

8

and then screening his calls, he gets to make up some great ego-saving reason I didn't answer. Maybe my ex called and we got back together. Maybe I was too drunk and forgot I'd given out my number and it's nothing personal that I'm not answering. Maybe…whatever. *Anything* is better than the truth.

But the real reason I don't like to give the flat-out rejection is the other way this can go down. I say, "No, I don't think so" or in some other way reject a guy and I get, "Whatever. Not like you're that hot anyway." Or "Whatever, bitch." Or any variation on "I wasn't really interested in you and you're ugly, stupid, and/or dumb."

Seriously. Happens to every woman at some point.

Some guy who a minute before wanted to spend more time with her is suddenly insulting and rude and telling her how he wouldn't hook up with her if she was the last woman on earth and how he was just trying to do some charity work or…

Whatever. Fragile little ego that can't handle rejection.

Sadly it's happened often enough to me and my friends over the years that it isn't even a surprise. (And, no, I'm not the type to pretend I like a guy to get him to buy me drinks or to in any way lead him on if I'm not interested. I will talk to a man who approaches me, but half the time I'm batting away any sort of flirtatious comments or attempts to touch me, so this is not some situation where I gave the guy the wrong impression unless you think I did that by acknowledging that he existed.)

Now, granted, this scenario often happens much earlier in the conversation (why men think a woman walking down the street has nothing better to do than stop and let them chat her up, I will never know), but it can happen at any point if the guy is that kind of guy.

Fortunately, scenario number two happens less often now that I'm older, uglier, and bitchier, but it still does happen. You would be genuinely surprised by the number of men who go from wanting to sleep with a woman to calling her names in the space of thirty seconds. Like the fact that she isn't willing to hook up with them is some sort of personal attack and affront to their ego.

Don't be that guy, by the way.

A woman doesn't want to give you her number? Move on. She doesn't want to talk to you? Move on. There are other, better women for you out there. Spend your time and energy finding them.

Also, now is a good time to remind you that your biggest enemy in finding a woman to date or marry or whatever you're looking for, is your fellow man. Because *you* may be great. You may be interesting and relatively attractive and worth her checking out. But you have to get through all the bullshit other men have thrown at her to get her to see that. And if you do anything to remind her of those creepers she's had to deal with in the past— like call her a name or treat her like a game to be won— you're done. She'll move on.

So anyway. Back to the point. Just because some woman gave you her number, doesn't mean she actually wants to see you again. Sad, but true.

ENTER THE BOYFRIEND

This is also the stage when a mysterious boyfriend can suddenly appear. You try to talk to a woman and she says, "Sorry, I have a boyfriend."

Or you're having a great conversation with a woman, you ask for her number, and she says, "Sorry, but my boyfriend doesn't like me to give out my number to strange guys."

Or you get her number or her agreement to go out sometime but when you follow-up she suddenly drops a boyfriend into the conversation like she didn't understand that you were asking her on a date, not trying to be her friend.

Does she have a boyfriend?

Maybe. But probably not.

(Ironic that women tend to make up boyfriends in these scenarios whereas a lot of men seem to forget they have a girlfriend in the same scenario, which is maybe why it works so well.)

The fake boyfriend is one of my go-to excuses for not engaging with a guy who's showing interest when I'm not feeling it. Or for backing out of getting together with someone I've changed my mind about. Especially if it's someone I don't know well but can expect to see again, like someone who hits on me at work.

I'll give you an example. Many, many years ago I worked at a bookstore. A guy who worked somewhere in the mall came in and we talked a little. I helped him find whatever book he was looking for and was nice and sweet, which I generally am to strangers, especially at work.

The next day he came back, hovered around nervously for quite some time, and finally got up the urge to ask if I'd like to maybe get a water or something sometime.

(Side note: First, if you want to ask a woman out, don't hover. Just do it. Hovering won't make her more likely to say yes, but it might make her say no if she notices that you're doing it, which I usually do. Also, unless there's some cool ironic joke you two have going on about drinking water, don't ask a woman out for a water. Even if that's all *you* drink, don't ask her out for a water. Ask her out for a coffee and when you get there order your water and let her order whatever it is she drinks.)

So there I was at work, knowing I'd see the guy around.

I didn't want to hurt his feelings, because he was one of those quiet shy types who took ten minutes building up his courage. But I also knew he was not going to be a good fit for me.

(Another side note: Most men who meet me in real life think that I'm very nice. And I am in many ways. Especially to the shy, awkward types. I'm not going to be rude or insulting to a guy like that. I will smile and talk about whatever they want to talk about and make the

YOU HAVE A DATE, DON'T F IT UP

situation as comfortable as possible for both of us while it lasts. But I *know* that a man like that will not do well with me. Because when I'm angry, men like that want to make it better. But what they need to do is get out of my way until I get over myself. So I don't date those types. It's too cruel to put them through that.)

Anyway. He asked me out. And, not wanting to just reject him, I said, "yeah, sure, but I really can't talk right now" hoping that non-committal response and blow-off would end things.

It didn't. He was back the next day asking when my break was.

Enter the boyfriend.

I said I really couldn't do anything that day because I'd been up late the night before talking to my boyfriend who was going to school on the East coast and it had made me late for work, so I was skipping my break to make up for it.

He fled. And I never saw him again.

I felt horrible. But…It did save me from the whole, "you are not a good fit for me" conversation.

That was not the first time I'd manufactured a boyfriend and it wasn't the last. It works, because most men will back off if they hear a woman is in a relationship. (Not all, though. There's the "Well we can just be friends" guys who are either smooth enough to know it can be a lie or who think they can charm a woman away from any man if given the opportunity. But that kind of guy is easy to straight up reject because he rarely takes it personally and he's on to the next woman within minutes.)

So what do you do if she suddenly mentions a boyfriend?

Nothing.

Move on to someone who is actually interested in dating you. Same goes for a woman who is suddenly so busy with work or friends that she just can't possibly fit you into her schedule anytime soon.

True or not, it doesn't matter. She isn't interested enough to bother with. And no woman is so amazing and wonderful and perfect that you need to waste your time trying to push through that. Just move on.

BEFORE YOU GET TOO DISCOURAGED…

By now you should realize that women often (and this is more for in-person conversations than online dating) will say yes to going on a date when they don't really mean yes.

But sometimes it goes the other way.

Sometimes a woman does want to go out with you but she genuinely is busy, or she does give you the wrong number by accident, or your email gets sent to her spam folder and she never even knows you reached out.

A good friend of mine has been dating a woman for a couple of years now, but when they first met she told him she couldn't get together for a couple of weeks because things at work were really busy. It wasn't that she wasn't interested. It just so happened she had a two-week work trip planned and couldn't squeeze time out of the couple of days she had free before the trip.

He could've written her off and assumed she really just didn't want to see him. But by hanging in there and playing it cool, he's now in a very happy relationship.

So don't get too cynical about all of this.

Just don't pin your hopes on one woman this early in the game. Keep looking around and be open to meeting someone else.

And with the woman who seems to be blowing you off? Try once, try twice, and then move on. If she circles back your way a little bit later and you don't have anything better in the works, give her another chance.

(Or not. There is nothing wrong with knowing how you want to be treated and only dealing with people who treat you that way. I recently had a guy cancel plans with me because he's too busy at work. Personally, that was a deal-breaker. I'm not interested in dating a man who lives for his work. And, quite frankly, I think the work excuse is usually code for "I'm just not that into you.")

Anyway. Don't always assume that because she didn't jump all over you or because something went wrong that she isn't interested.

Let me give you an example.

A while back I went out to meet some college friends for drinks. A buddy of one of the guys I knew dropped by and joined us. He ended up sitting next to me and we flirted back and forth for a couple hours. When it was time to leave, he offered to give me a ride home. I said sure. He drove me home.

When we pulled up outside my place, he said, "We should get together sometime."

And I said, "Yeah, sure, I'd like that," and then I got out of the car and went inside.

Sounds good, right?

One little problem.

The guy didn't have my number. Now, if I'd been really, really interested in him I would've probably nailed him down on some details of when/where this was going to happen (like, "Yeah, sure. Have you seen the latest

Jason Statham movie? Because I'm dying to see it.") Or at least I would have made sure he had my number in his phone before I got out of the car.

But, even though I'd done the "yeah, sure" thing and left before he could get my number, he wasn't down for the count at that point. He'd just run into twenty-plus years' worth of ingrained instinct. At this point in my life, shrugging guys off is something I do without even thinking about it.

(If I actually like a guy, I have to fight myself to not do that. And I often have to give it a bit of thought and then come back to him later, because my immediate reaction is almost always "just leave me alone, please.")

Where he "failed" is in not following up with our mutual friend to get my number. Or, better yet, emailing me, because we'd both been part of an email chain where we all arranged to meet up.

Of course, I could've done the same thing. I had his email, too. But I didn't. Because I wasn't *that* interested in him.

But don't assume it's over just because of something like that. If you're really interested and you have a way to do so without being creepy (we'll touch on that later), give it another try to make sure it wasn't a simple miscommunication.

WHAT IF SHE DOES ACTUALLY SEEM INTERESTED?

So let's say you got her number and she actually answered when you called or texted. Or you messaged her about going out and she said she'd like that.

Are you free and clear now? Is this going to result in a date?

Oh, hell no.

You are in the no-date-yet danger zone. Now you have to successfully negotiate all the details of a date without losing her. This is a point where things can go wrong fast.

You'd think it isn't a big deal. All you have to agree to is where to get together and when. How hard can that be?

You'd be surprised.

There are sooo many ways things can fall apart at this point, it isn't even funny.

But first let's take a moment to remind you of something I discussed in the other books that we haven't touched on yet: Women are not some one-size-fits-all sort of Barbie doll. There are no clear-cut rules you can apply to all women in all situations. Some women will like a man who takes charge and knows what he wants. (Like me.) Some would find that kind of guy overbearing and obnoxious. (Also sometimes me. Ha!)

So. Even though we're going to talk about how things can fall apart at this stage, keep in mind that if you know this woman better than I do and don't think what I'm saying here makes sense for dealing with her, then don't do it. Follow your gut.

If she's very particular about things and willing to communicate that to you, listen and follow her direction. But if you don't have a good read on her yet? Or think she's the kind to agree to plans without much fuss? Then follow the approach I'm about to recommend.

Also, before we begin, keep in mind there's a bit of a ticking clock between when a woman agrees to go out with you and when that date needs to happen. Personally, unless there are some very good reasons for it—like one of you is out of the country or the state—I wouldn't allow more than a week to pass between suggesting a date and actually having it.

Why? Well, first, she could meet someone else, go out with them, and like them enough to no longer be interested in you. Second, it gets tricky to keep up the momentum of the conversation when you can't get together. And, third, if you don't make it a priority to see her, you're not signaling to her that you're genuinely interested. What you're doing is showing her that there are a lot of things in your life more important than going out with her.

It's possible she's the reason for the delay. In which case you should ask yourself how interested she is in you? And is it worth holding out for a woman who puts that many things before you? Because you need to value yourself if you legitimately want to find long-term happiness.

I know too many men willing to settle for less than they deserve because (a) the woman is really attractive and they let that blind them to how miserably she treats them or (b) they're so worried about being alone that they'll settle for anything they can get.

Don't do that to yourself.

Whatever you look like, whatever you do for a job, whatever your interests are, there is a woman out there who will make you happy and be glad to be with you. Find her. And don't settle until you do.

Alright, enough of that.

So you're interested and she's interested, and now all you have to do is agree on the particulars and not f up between here and the actual date.

Let's spend a couple chapters discussing where you can potentially go wrong at this point and some strategies to get past them.

WHERE AND WHEN TO MEET

Believe it or not, things can completely derail over an inability to agree on where and when to meet. If you think about it, it's actually a negotiation. You two have to work together to determine what you're going to do, where you're going to do it, and when. And that isn't always easy.

Now, I understand that this is a first date and you want to be somewhat accommodating to your date's interests. I get that. But I would recommend that the best approach here is to take charge.

By that I mean, you say something like this: "What do you say to going to [insert thing you guys talked about and you know she's interested in]. I'm free Saturday, if that works for you."

If she likes your idea and is also free Saturday, you're 90% of the way there in one message. All she has to do is say, "Sounds great! Want to meet at noon in the south parking lot?"

Of course, it rarely goes that smoothly.

Instead she'll say "Sounds great," and then you'll have to suggest when to meet and will probably forget to suggest where and there'll be a good five emails exchanged before you've nailed down the details. But it's still better than the alternative.

The alternative goes something like this:

You: "So what do you want to do? Dinner maybe? Or we could go to that exhibit you mentioned."

Her: "Yeah, dinner sounds good. Where were you thinking?"

You: "What about Hennesy's?"

Her: "Which one?"

You: "The one on 16th and Blake."

Her: "Oh, yeah. That works."

You: "Great. How about Friday?"

Her: "Sure. What time?"

You: "Six?"

Her: "I can't do that early. How about seven?"

You: "Okay."

And that's assuming you immediately agreed on what, when, and where. Look at that conversation again. Do you see how many times you gave her a chance to end the conversation? Or for the conversation to derail?

Think about how this plays out if you're both busy people who aren't constantly connected to your phone/computer/whatever so there's a delay between each message. That string of texts or emails could take three days. And if it takes too long you run into the situation where you're trying to make plans for the next day which is generally a no-no.

The vague approach allows too much room for one or the other of you to think things have gone wrong or that you're being ignored or that the other person isn't really that interested or for you to make some side comment that ends things completely.

That's why suggesting what, where, and when in the first message is a better approach. The shorter the distance between her saying yes and the actual date, the better.

But, because you don't know her well and this is a first date, you should still remain flexible. If she comes back and says, "I really don't like Thai, but I'd be up for Mexican," great. Suggest a specific Mexican place.

But in every single message, be trying to lock down the details and close the deal. Vague "sure, maybe, whatever" communication will never get you where you want to go, which is on an actual date.

AN ASIDE: THE RULES BEHIND SETTING UP A DATE

So there's this book called *The Rules* and some of the advice in there has maybe trickled down into women's subconscious. It isn't so much playing games as wanting to be respected and knowing that certain times mean more than others and that agreeing to go on a date with almost no notice conveys a certain message.

I've never read the book and I'm not even sure all the little rules I carry around in my head originated there, but I'll give you a brief rundown of the ones I seem to apply without realizing it.

- A dinner date is "more serious" than a lunch date
- A breakfast date is not something you do on as a first date
- A date for a Friday night or a Saturday night is "more serious" than a date for any other night of the week
- A date involving a meal is "more serious" than a date involving drinks, even if that drink date evolves into a date that includes a meal

- Dinner and a movie is a sort of standard clichéd date, but rare these days in my experience
- Early dates should not involve other family members
- Early dates should also not involve friends
- You generally shouldn't ask or agree to go on a date with only a day's notice. (It implies you have no life or are willing to cancel existing plans for this person.)
- If you're older than about twenty, no date should involve a fast food restaurant.
- A man who chooses some incredibly expensive restaurant for a first date is trying too hard.
- Chain restaurants are best avoided, but seem to be a far too common choice.

Those are the ones I can think of off the top of my head. If you look at them you can see where you might get into trouble. You ask a woman on Thursday if she wants to meet you for dinner on Friday and you're not only asking for prime date real estate (dinner on a Friday), you're also asking her to agree to a date with almost no notice.

If I recall what I've heard correctly, if you want a date for a weekend, you should have plans made by Wednesday at the absolute latest. Now, does this mean she won't agree to a Friday date if you ask on Thursday? No. I think I've done it. But there is this little calculus she does in her head when you do that and it involves how interesting you are, how much she cares about perception, etc.

And you really do need to finalize the date a day or two in advance. I recently went through a scenario where on a Friday morning we had discussed meeting on a Sunday and then the guy didn't get back to me on Friday afternoon or Saturday. By the time I woke up Sunday, he wasn't part of my plans for the day, because I'm not going to sit around on the off chance that this guy who couldn't finalize plans is going to come through at the last minute. Nope.

(Turns out in that case that he thought he'd sent an email but he hadn't and we didn't resolve the miscommunication until Monday when he followed up. Unfortunate, but didn't prevent me from mentally writing him off by the time Sunday rolled around.)

So, when suggesting a date, keep the above in mind. She's more likely to agree to a date that you set up a few days in advance that is less serious. So, afternoon coffee on a Sunday that you schedule by Thursday is more likely to get a yes than a fancy dinner on Friday that you try to schedule on Thursday.

DON'T SAY STUPID SHIT

Alright. Back to ways you can mess things up before the actual date.

Even though this woman has agreed to go out on a date with you, that doesn't mean she will. Especially if you slip up and say something really stupid or offensive to her before the actual date.

Unless you're frickin' gorgeous and accomplished and a man any woman would kill to be with (which makes me wonder why you're reading this) a woman will walk away if you offend her or say something that makes her realize you are not someone she wants to waste time on.

(Well, at least I will.)

I'll give you an example.

Now, granted, this guy already had a strike against him for lying about his age on his profile, but I had still agreed to go out with him. So we were doing the back and forth about where to meet up. He went with the, "Hey, where do you think you'd want to meet? Somewhere down south maybe?" approach.

And then we exchanged email after email after email with nothing decided. Keep in mind here, that I try to be very flexible at this stage and let the man "take charge" and choose the actual place. So, I said something like, "That works for me. Where were you thinking?" etc. etc.

But we kept going back and forth and not settling on plans.

This went on for a few days until finally I said something like, "How about we meet at X restaurant on such-and-such street at 6 on Wednesday?"

To which he responded, "Wow. I can see why that guy thought you were a dominatrix."

Really?

I try to finalize plans and suddenly I'm some whip-wielding woman in latex?

Now, a little context here. When I'd first joined this particular dating site some guy had messaged me about how he was looking for an older woman to take a firm hand with him. (I kid you not.) So I'd had a little back and forth with this guy I was trying to arrange a date with about that happening in a "you wouldn't believe what women have to deal with on here" sort of way.

His little comment about me being a dominatrix was not funny. Because it came off as a "back in your place" sort of comment. Like my trying to finalize plans was in some way offensive.

Not the kind of guy I was going to waste more time on.

I mean, seriously. You want to insult me before we've ever even met? No. I'll stay at home and watch Luke Cage with my pup rather than waste two hours of my life with you, thank you very much.

So don't get cute. And don't say stupid shit. It's too hard to fix when you're not face-to-face.

If you wouldn't make that kind of joke or comment on a job interview, don't make it online or via text while trying to set up a date. What you think you said and the tone you think you said it in, may not be how it comes across. Put your best foot forward until you're together in person and you can read her reactions.

DON'T GET COMFY

Another reason I recommend moving from asking for a date to the actual date in less than a week is because it doesn't let you slip up and get too comfortable. Honestly, with online dating, I think you need to move from match to date within about two weeks if you can. Even faster than that if possible.

Especially if you've just ended a long-term relationship. It's far too easy to fall back into your old patterns from your relationship and get too comfortable with this woman before you should be.

Honestly, and it sounds stupid, the more you treat this like a potential job interview, the better off you'll be. It'll remind you that your goal right now is to impress her enough to get the "offer." In this case, the date.

Let's walk through a few real-world examples from my oh-so-wonderful dating past where guys got a little too comfy too soon.

The first couple come from a point in time a few years back when I was living in New Zealand but moving back to the States. During the last month I was in New Zealand I figured I'd get a head start on things by opening an online dating account in the States, so that when I returned I'd have someone to go out with right away.

(Not recommended. Too long of a time lag between matching with someone and seeing them in person as you're about to see.)

So I met a couple of guys who showed some promise. And, because I wasn't there to meet up with them, we kept exchanging messages over the course of that month.

The first guy slowly moved from suggesting that we go out when I was back in town, to suggesting that we have our first date at his house, to talking about how that date could be in his basement snuggled up on the couch watching movies.

Think about this for a second. A guy I had never met before in person, who as far as I knew could be a serial killer, wanted me to come to his house and hang out in his basement.

No.

No, no, no.

Way too intimate for a first date.

And, honestly, unless you're trying to set up a date with your best friend's sister or someone equivalent, you need to keep in mind that you don't know this woman either. You don't want her to know where you live yet. Not until you've determined she isn't going to cut up your bunny rabbit and leave it cooking on the stove. (That's from a Glenn Close movie for those of you too young to remember…)

Because this guy got way too comfy too fast, I went from being willing to meet him for a coffee to never wanting to see him in real life, ever, ever, ever. (There were a few other little red flags there, too, but that was the final straw for me.) I'm sure he spent too much time reading my messages and looking at my photos and thought he knew me. He didn't.

The second guy got too comfortable in a different way. He started talking about things you just don't tell someone you're not in a relationship with. Like how he'd played softball the day before and his shoulder was really hurting him and he'd had to ice it and put Bengay on and how now that he was older he found that he just didn't get around as well anymore and…

Do you think that's sexy? Or appealing in any way? Do you think talking about your aches and pains will make a woman like you more?

It won't. I mean, sure, that's your life, but maybe don't share that before the first date?

Remember, think job interview. Would you tell a prospective employer about your aches and pains? No. No you would not.

A friend of mine, who is a little less rigorous about screening out the crazies (and actually willing to share her phone number and personal email before meeting someone in person which I will not do if I can avoid it), had a few more examples of men who got too comfy too soon.

One guy texted her "Good morning, Beautiful" every single morning leading up to their date.

They'd never met in person. Never had a date.

Maybe he thought it was sweet. Or cute.

It wasn't.

That right there is downright creepy. Don't do that.

Remember, until you meet this woman in person you're just a weird stranger on the internet or some dude who hit on her at the bar. You could be anyone. All of your pictures and likes and dislikes could be complete fabrications.

(I think my friend actually went on that date, but I wouldn't have, because that would've been a sign to me of a potential crazy stalker type and I don't go there if I can avoid it. Been there, done that.)

The other one that was a way-too-soon thing was the guy who sent her a Facebook friend request. He didn't ask if he could do it or talk to her about it beforehand either. He just used her email to track her down on Facebook and then let her know he'd done so by sending the friend request. (The reason the email I use for dating is not an email I use for anything else.)

Now, this could just be a generational thing. I'm sure there are many twenty-something women out there who wouldn't bat an eye at it, but I certainly do.

I say far too much shit on Facebook for me to be friends with just anyone. Also, first dates sometimes don't go well and I really don't need some guy I don't want to see again being my Facebook friend.

So hold off until at least the second date on that. Perhaps even longer.

I have another friend who is now happily married with twins, who dated her now-husband for at least nine months before they became FB friends. And it's a good thing, too. He didn't need to know that she'd posted about freezing her eggs or about the dude she'd hit on at the gym a few weeks before she met him. And maybe she didn't need to see whatever dumbass posts he'd made the year before.

They are very happy now, but that might not have happened if they'd had full access to each other's' FB posts from day one. So, chill out a bit.

And remember: No matter how great the conversations have been, don't let yourself get too comfortable. At least not until you get that first date under your belt. Remind yourself that you are strangers and that you want to impress her at this stage.

KEEP YOUR COOL

Let's say you somehow snagged the number of a woman you think is way out of your league. And you are on cloud 9. You just can't get over how amazingly lucky you are to have a shot at this woman. I mean, she's gorgeous. And she gave you her number and even answered the phone when you called.

You cannot let her know this.

You need to keep your cool. Do not show her how much out of your league you think she is.

No gushing.

No over the top ridiculousness.

The following is a true story even though it doesn't seem like it should be.

Back in college I was walking through the main quad one day and some guy stopped me to tell me how much he liked my arms. (As you might have figured out by now, men say weird things to women all the time. Or at least they do to me.)

Anyway. I was in a good mood so I talked to him. And when he asked for my number, I gave it to him.

He gave me his as well. Written on, I believe, a five-dollar bill. That should've been a huge red flag, but sadly, it wasn't the first time a man had written his number on money and given it to me. Still. (Don't do that, BTW. It's weird and she's far more likely to spend the money than keep it.)

Anyway. Good mood. Gave him my number. Got his. He called. I answered.

And we proceeded to have one of the most bizarre conversations I have ever had in my life. It seems he worked for a jewelry importer, so he told me that instead of bringing me roses for our first date he was going to bring me jewelry. And somewhere in that conversation he also told me he'd let me drive his car. And that when I went home for the summer from college he'd buy me a fax machine so we could keep in touch. (This was a long time ago. Cellphones existed but they were about three times the size of your hand and weighed a good five pounds.) I think he also mentioned flying me to Bangladesh to meet his family. It was either on that call or the next time he called.

I quickly moved from somewhat amused to "oh hell no."

This guy was way too over the top.

And when I tried to point out all the reasons we weren't compatible—I deliberately chose the opposite interests in everything from music to movies—he didn't care. He just thought I was really beautiful and that's all that mattered to him.

Don't do this. Don't even do a toned-down version of this.

Play it cool. If the woman is the right one for you, you do not need to bribe her or buy her or do ridiculous things to impress her. You should approach any woman you want to date as if you're an equal and you deserve her time and attention. Make her believe that you will improve her life by being in it. You do that by being confident in who you are and what you bring to the table.

So none of this desperate over-the-top stuff. Keep your cool.

Now, maybe you disagree with me on this. You have lots of money and you know that's your main source of appeal for women.

Okay.

You might want to work on that, by the way. Even if she sticks around long enough to marry you she'll probably divorce you at some point if that's all you bring to the table.

But let's talk this through.

Money *can be* an endearing quality to some women. But you don't have to be ridiculous about it. And if you are going to be flashing your cash to appeal to women, you need to make sure you're dealing with the type of woman who cares about that.

I'm not that woman. My alarm bells start going off the moment a man leans too heavily on how much he makes or has without offering anything else.

Other women are different. They love the thought of a man spending hundreds or thousands of dollars on them when he barely knows them.

But until you know what kind of woman you're dealing with? Hold back a bit.

Also, keep in mind that a woman whose interest can essentially be bought with money is a woman who can be lost to a man with more money. And know that if you're with a woman like that and you hit a downturn financially you will not only be broke you will also be alone.

Those types of relationships do work, so if that's how you want to play it more power to you, just know that leaning too heavily on how much you make can drive away women who are looking for more substance than that.

And, no matter what, with any woman, have enough confidence to believe that you deserve to be with her. (If you don't believe that, reconsider where you're focusing your efforts. Better to aim a little lower and be secure in yourself than aim too high and spend your life a nervous wreck waiting for your house of cards to fall down on your head when she realizes how much better than you she is. Ideally you both think you got a good deal.)

DON'T ARGUE

Another way you can ruin things before you ever get to that first date is by arguing with your potential date over stupid shit.

Granted, sometimes two people are so incompatible that an argument is bound to happen, which to me means you really need to just walk away. I mean, honestly, if you can't set up a first date with someone without getting into a disagreement with them? That's not a good sign.

Again, going back to this job interview analogy, would you really argue with your future employer in your job interview? I hope not. Because unless you meet all of their needs and they know there is no one out there even close to comparing to you, you're not going to get that job. They'll move on and find someone more pleasant to work with.

Same with dating. If she has a more pleasant choice and you aren't head and shoulders above her other options, she'll choose him instead.

Don't argue over stupid shit. You have a whole relationship for that.

Here's what happened to me. It's a second date example, but the principle remains the same.

A guy I'd gone out with messaged me about going out again. I said sure and that I was kind of craving brunch, so maybe we could get together on Sunday for brunch somewhere.

Seems simple, right? What's there to argue about there? Well…

He replied that "bunch" sounded like a great idea and then proceeded to suggest a place that didn't actually serve it. When I pointed out to him that the place he'd suggested didn't serve brunch (as I recall it was a very good Mexican place, but definitely not a brunch place), and sent him a link to an article on top brunch places in the area, he argued with me about it by informing me that the place he'd suggested opened at 11.

Problem is, brunch isn't just a meal you have at a certain time of day. It also involves a certain type of food. And guacamole and tacos are not part of that. At least not last time I checked.

So there we were. I had actually been okay with going out with him again (not thrilled and giddy, but okay), but then we got into some ridiculous back and forth about brunch of all things.

If he'd been right about it, I would've conceded the point and maybe, maybe we would've managed to make it to that second date. But he wasn't. And he kept pressing the point and calling it "bunch" and suggesting places that weren't brunch places even though I'd sent him the link with a list of brunch places.

So, instead of going out with him again, I told him I was swamped with work and moved on. And, because he'd lost my interest, that was true. This was a point in my life where I was traveling every single week, Monday through Friday, for work. It didn't take much for me to decide that a man who'd argue with me over "bunch" was not a man who deserved any part of those few precious days I had at home each week.

See, here's the deal. Until you've got someone hooked (think fishing, it's a good analogy), you need to handle them with a bit of care or they'll wriggle free and go about their merry way without you.

And again, going back to the job analogy: Until you've been hired and onboarded and shown that company that you are a rock star that they can't afford to lose, you don't have any sort of job security whatsoever.

You could be the world's greatest and they'll never know if you f it up before you get a chance to show them.

So play nice. Let things slide.

You can be an argumentative asshole later in the relationship when she thinks you're cute and adorable and cranky like an Ewok. At the pre-date stage you pull that shit and she'll just think you're a jerk and move on to the next one.

(And there's *always* a next one…)

WHERE TO GO ON YOUR FIRST DATE

Alright, so we've resolved that you're not going to be a dumbass between the time she says she'll go out with you and when you actually meet up. Now, what should you *do* for that first date?

My personal opinion is that you shouldn't spend a lot of money. My best first date ever involved cheap beer, a few games of pool, and some late night food at Denny's. It's far more about getting to know each other than being impressed.

(For me. Remember, all women are unique and some will want the fancy schmancy dinner. But don't splash out on a fancy date unless you know that's the kind of woman you're dealing with and you're interested enough to do it. Bottom line here: Don't spend money just because you feel insecure. Okay?)

So, my recommendation is no dinner at Morton's and no hundred-dollar event tickets unless you have season tickets or won them in a contest or something.

Now, the classics these days, especially for someone you've only met online, seem to be meeting for coffee or meeting for a drink. And while there's nothing wrong with those, I kind of hate them.

For two reasons: One, especially with meeting for drinks, it's never really meeting for drinks. It's meeting for a drink so I can determine if you look like your photo and can carry a conversation at which point I suggest we go to dinner somewhere. I hate that. Because I can pass the damned drink test, thank you very much.

But your assumption that I've kept my entire night free so I can pass that little test and we can move on from there?

Eh. I often make plans for dinner with a friend after a drink date because if a guy asked me for a drink, that's what he's getting.

(As I write these books I am continually reminded why I am still single. But just think about it this way: If you can get past someone as obnoxious as me, you'll do fabulous with 90% of women.)

By the way, the way to not annoy me with that sort of thing is to say something like. "Why don't we meet up for a drink and then see where things go from there?"

The other reason I don't like the drink or coffee date is it's so boring and clichéd. Yes, it does give you a chance to talk to someone, so that's a positive. But it also shows a complete lack of originality.

I prefer dates that involve doing something. For example, I've had a couple good first dates where we played pool. It lets you have that drink, but it also involves a fun activity that lets you flirt easily, too.

I also had a decent date where we took our dogs for a walk around a big lake. It let us talk, but also get some exercise in, and, bonus in my book, I didn't have to choose between some guy I didn't know and my dog.

Another good one was meeting up at one of those bars that have old-school video games like Ms. Pac-Man.

We got to have our drinks but also played some video games at the same time.

If you do go for an activity date, I'd recommend something that still allows you to interact one-on-one so you can talk and get to know each other. And it should be in a public place.

There are a lot of crazies in this world. Some people don't think about these things, but you really should. For you and for them. Remember, men aren't the only ones who can become obsessive stalkers.

And do something fun or exciting if you can. That little adrenaline rush will get associated with you which is a good thing.

Also, choose a date that shows off your more positive traits or competence. Now is not the time to try to do something for the first time or that you're really bad at. Like bowling or indoor skydiving.

If something came up in your conversations and you can personalize the first date to the woman's interests, do it. A friend of mine and her now-husband had a first date where they went looking for a children's playground because of something they had discussed when they were getting to know each other online.

(That kind of a conversation also makes a nice opening to suggest the date in the first place. You know, "So you love roller coasters? There's a great old one at the amusement park right down the street. We should go check it out sometime.")

I would also recommend that you choose an activity that's an hour or two at most. Half an hour if you're not sure of the person.

And do be flexible about keeping the date going if it's going well. With someone you met in real life that's probably more likely to happen than with someone you met online.

But don't read anything into it if they have to cut the date short or can't extend it. Especially if they have kids or pets. Some people are up against hard deadlines for babysitters or pet sitters.

Chances are, if you haven't met in person, that first date is really just filling in for the conversation you would've had if you'd met at a bar. It's possible you'll meet and click and just keep talking and talking and talking, but it's more likely you'll meet, click, and agree to see each other again soon.

ONE FINAL NOTE ON COMMUNICATING BEFORE THE FIRST DATE

These days I tend to meet men through online dating. And my policy in those situations is to generally avoid giving out my phone number or my email if I can. The site is there to allow us to communicate without getting too much into each other's space, and I think that's a perfectly fine way to reach someone, so that's what I stick to.

I might, on the day of or the day before a date, provide my phone number, or more likely my email, in case something goes wrong and they're running late or can't find me where we're supposed to meet.

But I really don't want the guy to use that to text or call me before the date.

That sounds awful, but fact of the matter is, a guy I've never met in person hasn't earned the right to intrude on my life that much.

I realize some people take a very different approach to this and want to talk on the phone or email or text a lot before they meet up, so all I would say here is to let the woman set the tone and pace. If you ask for her number and she says she doesn't want to provide it yet, don't read anything into that. She might've just had some creepy experiences like my friend did and has learned from them.

If she does give you her phone number and you send a text or call and she doesn't text you back or call you back, then don't keep trying. And if she takes a long time to respond, then maybe back off.

The slowed response is one of my more subtle ways to slow a guy down. If that doesn't work I often will do the "Wow, you seem to have a lot of time on your hands. Sure you actually have a job?" sort of comment to get a guy to slow it down a bit.

When things are flowing smoothly between you, you'll know it. It's a bit like volleying in tennis. You have to both be engaged in the conversation and willing to go back and forth to keep it going.

I remember on one of the sites I was on there was a chat option, and some guy I was supposed to meet up with a day or two later suddenly sent me a chat message while I was online. Well, that wasn't what I really wanted to be doing. I was on there dealing with messages I'd received from other guys while watching a show I wanted to see (this was pre-DVR days for me), so I was slow to respond and we never really got into a conversational flow since there were a good five minutes between each of my responses.

On the other hand, there was a guy I liked who I would communicate with via Facebook's chat option. The minute he was on there and sent me a hello message we'd start talking back and forth like it was a real in-person conversation. As soon as he finished what he was typing, I'd respond. Or vice versa. We were in synch.

So if you send a text or chat message and you're sitting there for a minute or two straight with no response?

That's not a good conversation. Let it go and just focus on getting to that first date, because things can change drastically once you've met in person and really clicked.

THE FIRST DATE:
HOW NOT TO SCREW IT UP

Okay. Let's say you survived the landmines of trying to get from "yes" to the actual date.

You're still not in the clear. There are so many things that can go wrong on a first date. Some people approach them with a bunch of hope and optimism, looking to meet "the one." But lots approach them with a certain amount of cynicism looking for those hidden signs that you're a train wreck they need to avoid. (Guess which one I am...)

So this is going to seem like a laundry list of complaints. But it isn't. Just think how you'd feel if someone did these things on your date. Would you really want to go out again with a woman who showed up late, in a crappy outfit that looked like she didn't even try, and then texted with her friends the whole time? No? Well, then don't do that yourself.

The golden rule really does apply here: Do unto others as you'd have them do unto you. Follow that as your guide and nine times out of ten you'll do well.

(The only time that isn't true is when we're talking about the creeper thing. Sadly, I know a number of men who'd love a woman to be overly sexually aggressive with them on a first date. But the reverse is generally not true, so don't do that, not unless she starts it.)

Alright. Let's dive in, shall we?

Be On Time

Actually, be a little early. Better that than late. You never know what's going to go wrong on the way there so it's always good to build in a bit of a cushion. You really don't want to leave some poor girl sitting around wondering where you are and looking at every guy who walks through the door to see if it's you. That's not a great way to start things off.

And, if you are early, keep an eye out for her so that when she walks in she isn't stuck wondering which of the ten guys sitting alone around the bar are the one she's supposed to meet. It's polite, for starters, and you also don't need her seeing some hot guy at the bar and then seeing you and feeling that little moment of disappointment that she isn't meeting him instead.

(I kid. Sort of.)

Don't Hang Back Until She Buys Her Drink

I have had this happen at least three times. I've arranged to meet a guy for a drink, arrived, looked around, thought I saw him but wasn't sure, so decided I'd order a drink while I waited for him to arrive. In the meantime, it turned out it was him and he did recognize me and moved closer, but hung back long enough for me to order my drink and pay for it. Only then did he say my name and introduce himself.

Now, clearly, in each instance, the guy recognized me. Two out of three times I was the only woman there. But yet he didn't bother to step in until I'd paid for my own drink.

It didn't end things right then. Two out of three of those, we went on to have dinner and he did pay for dinner. But it was something I noticed and it was a little x in the negative column. And none of the three resulted in a second date.

See, here's why you don't do this. Because by hanging back, you're forcing her to look around the room to find you. (This is also why you should be on time.) And when she has to do that—look at every guy sitting alone long enough to determine if it's you—chances are one of those guys is going to take that as an invitation to come over and say hi.

Think about it. How often do women walk into bars and look around at every single guy long enough for them to notice? Not often and not unless they're looking to be hit on, because that is what will happen.

That's why I order the drink. It buys some time for the guy I'm meeting to recognize me and come over. But just because she started the process of getting a drink doesn't mean you then hang back and let her buy it. As we'll see next, I think the guy should pay for at least the first drink or meal.

Pay

There's a lot of discussion that goes on around this, and I get that. Dating is expensive for men. If you go on twenty dates in a month—which one of my guy friends did when he was single and living in New York City—it can really add up. Especially if you're going through lots of first dates with women that aren't great fits. (May I suggest that you pay less attention to a woman's appearance and more to her personality in the future?)

And it can get tempting to not want to pay. Or to ask to split the dinner tab. But if it's that much of an issue for you, you're better off choosing dates that don't cost money. A walk around a lake, for example. A free concert in the park. A free art exhibit. Whatever.

But if you choose a date that involves spending money, then pay. At least for the first drink or the meal.

Which does not mean the woman should expect you to do so. I always plan on paying for myself, but I'm never impressed when I have to.

Now, someone out there is thinking that in this age of equality, why should a man be the one who pays? And fair enough. I get that it can seem ridiculous. But as equal as men and women are these days, there's still something to be said for the man courting the woman.

And it's not like things are actually equal when it comes to dating. Women are in far more demand than men. With online dating I'd estimate that women probably get twenty or more messages from men for every one message a man gets from a woman. Same with being hit on in person. Men are far more likely to hit on women than women are to hit on men.

So fact of the matter is, you as a man are competing for this woman in a way that she's not competing for you. (At this point. She is competing, too. But it happens earlier in the process. Based on how she dresses and presents herself, men decide whether to hit on her or to hit on someone else. But at the date stage the tables are now turned and she gets to pick from the men who did approach her which ones she wants to keep seeing.)

So at the date stage, impressing your date and standing out from other men is something you should think about.

I don't know other women's pay-to-not-pay ratios, but in my experience it's been about 80% of men will pay and 20% will want to split the check. And I, fortunately, have yet to run into the guy who thinks I should pay or bails on me before the check arrives.

(And if some guy did leave me with the check? As in ordered a bunch of shit and then snuck off to the bathroom after the meal was over and disappeared on me? I'd pay my half and then encourage the restaurant to call the cops on him since he'd run out on his half of it and we hadn't agreed I was paying. And honestly, if a woman did that to a guy—snuck away after ordering a bunch of food—I'd say he had the right to do the same thing.)

Now, I *am* sensitive to these sorts of things, so if a guy I'm on a first date with buys the first round of drinks, I will offer to buy the next round. Or if he buys dinner, I will offer to buy dessert. And I mean it when I make that offer.

But I've learned through painful experience not to insist on doing so.

I had a great first (or maybe second, hard to tell in this situation) date with a guy that I'd known for a while that involved going dancing at a couple of bars. And, because my guy friends had busted my chops about how guys always have to pay and how unfair it is and how a woman should keep it even, I insisted on buying drinks at the second bar. He didn't want me to, he was fine paying, but I insisted.

After a few hours of salsa dancing we were all comfy cozy when the place closed. But we couldn't leave yet, because I had to close out my tab. Which took some time. And kinda killed the vibe. To this day I wonder how differently things might've gone if I'd just let him buy our drinks that night (he was paying cash).

So the best way I can phrase this is don't fight the flow. Pay if it's easier to do so, let her if it isn't. And don't get hung up on money being spent if there's really something there. Because it'll all even itself out in the end if there is something lasting between you.

If You Do Pay, Commit To It

I should add that if you are going to pay, do so immediately and without hesitation. When the check arrives, I will always reach for my wallet and offer to split it. Nine times out of ten, the guy says, "No, I've got it," and that's it before I can even pull my wallet out of my purse.

But I had one date that was so awkward about paying that he lost all points for doing so.

The check came. I reached for my wallet. I pulled out my wallet. I pulled out my credit card. I reached for the check.

All this time he's talking to me, but making no move towards the check and I'm wondering if he's going to expect me to pay and thinking that's not going to go over well.

Finally, when I put my hands on the check, he reached for it.

Then he took a while to read over it. And I'm sitting there wondering if he's calculating his half (don't do that— if you're going to split the check, just split it 50/50). Finally, he reached for his wallet and said he'd get it.

By letting me think for a good few minutes that he was going to make me pay or wanted to split it, he lost all goodwill that paying would've earned him. Don't do that.

The best approach is to not even give your date time to reach for her wallet. When the check comes, grab it immediately. If she offers to pay her share (which I would still do and sincerely mean it), tell her you've got it. And then if you need to, only after you've said you've got it, study it to make sure it's accurate. But don't study it before you've confirmed that you're paying.

And don't let her get so far that she's reaching for the check wondering if you even plan to pay your half.

Like I said before, you don't have to pay for her share. There's no requirement. But keep in mind that other men do pay and that's who you're up against. So if you want to split the check you better be bringing more to the table than other guys.

And I'll tell you just anecdotally from my own experience that the men I've gone out with who wanted to split the check were not the ones bringing more to the table. Each one I can think of was a man that I quite frankly wasn't that impressed with before the check arrived, and their wanting to split the check just confirmed things for me.

So do what you want, but don't be penny-wise and pound foolish. Don't lose the girl of your dreams because you wanted to save yourself $25.

Alright, back to some basics.

Dress Nice

You don't need to wear a suit and tie, especially if the occasion doesn't call for it. Jeans and a t-shirt are a perfectly fine choice for a casual date. But make sure that your clothes are clean, and there aren't any holes in them that aren't supposed to be there.

Also make sure your clothes fit you well and are appropriate to the occasion.

Many years ago I met a guy to play pool for a first date. It was not a surprise that we were going to be playing pool because we had very specifically agreed to do so and gone to a pool hall where the only thing to do was play pool.

He happened to wear a pair of jeans that were at least a size too big for him. Which meant that every single shot he took, he had to pull his pants back up afterwards. Now, this wasn't some hip-hop lothario pulling off that sort of gangster look. This was just a normal dude who wore a pair of jeans that didn't fit him well. And every single time he had to pull those pants up, it reminded me that he either hadn't thought much about what we were going to be doing on our date or didn't think much about his appearance or…I don't know.

Whatever the reason, it didn't help. And there wasn't enough about him to overcome the negative impression the poorly-fitting jeans gave.

The goal in dressing nice is to eliminate reasons for the woman to say no to you. You can go one step further and dress well enough to give her a reason to say yes. But, at a minimum, you should dress nice enough to eliminate that as a reason to reject you.

Also Don't Wear Anything Offensive

Now, I've never had this happen, but I could see it being an issue: Do not wear t-shirts or hats that are in some way offensive or off-putting.

A first date is not the time to wear your "making bacon" t-shirt that has two pigs going at it. Not unless you know what kind of woman you're dealing with and are damned sure she'll find it funny. Same with pot-themed clothes. (I'm in Colorado, I have to mention it.) Unless you know she's a pot-smoker herself, you probably don't want to lead with drug use.

And, since this is 2017 and our president is who he is, I wouldn't wear one of those red "Make American Great

Again" caps either. That's a good way to find yourself stood up.

Don't Be Rude To Others

Some guys do well at making a woman feel special and well-treated, but then turn around and are absolute assholes to everyone else. They insult the waiter, complain about everyone they know, and are generally jerks to everyone except the person they want something out of—their date.

Some women don't notice this, but I certainly do. And I privately wonder how long he'll be nice to me before he turns on me, too.

A subset of this is the guy who bashes his ex. I talked about this in the online dating books, but let's go over it again: When you talk negatively about your ex—maybe you call her an uptight bitch or say she was too immature for a relationship or use any of a number of other creative and offensive terms to describe her—you're basically telling the woman in front of you that there are circumstances under which a woman you loved and cared for enough to date and possibly marry can go from special and valued by you to whatever nasty terms you're using. Which means *she* can also go from someone you treat with love and respect to someone you hate and bad mouth to strangers.

Now, is it possible that your ex was too immature for a relationship? Sure. Or that she's a crazy psycho? Yeah. But is this date the place to bring that up? No.

If your prior relationship comes up in conversation, the best thing to do is say that it didn't work out. And then move on to some other topic. Focus on the moment and keep the past out of it. There will come a time when you should disclose all of that, but it's not when you're trying to make a good first impression.

(Again, I'm sort of assuming here that this is a woman you don't know already. My mom and my stepdad's first date broke all of the "rules" I'm telling you here, and they've been married over twenty years at this point. But they'd also known each other for a few months before their first date so a lot of that letting someone see that you're not a crazy psycho part of things had already been taken care of.)

Don't Talk About Your Ex

I mentioned already that you shouldn't insult your ex, but really, don't talk about them at all. I can't remember a single time when a guy talked about his ex that it was a good thing for the date.

Examples? Sure, why not.

I had one guy I went out with who was still clearly in love with his ex. He talked about how beautiful she was. He showed me a picture of her. When we dropped by his place he mentioned how she'd decorated it and what a wonderful job she'd done. Eventually, his ex-talk was a big part of why we ended. Because I didn't need to compete with a size two perfect woman who wasn't all the way out of his life.

If he'd instead focused on the moment and me, things would've gone a lot better for us.

Another guy I went on a date with talked about how his ex and he had broken up because she wanted kids, and he wasn't ready for that after five years of dating. He also mentioned that she'd wanted kids the whole time and that he'd never wanted them.

Well, if kids had been a high priority for me in finding someone, that would've ended things right then and there. Because, (a) he didn't want kids and (b) he'd revealed himself to be the kind of guy who would lie to a woman about it to keep her in the relationship. Maybe he'd changed since that relationship, but by talking about that and not giving any other information, he basically put a big red x on himself.

I also had a guy that was actually the opposite of that scenario. He talked about how every woman he dated seemed to want to get serious right away. Spent a good twenty minutes on the topic. Which was a bad thing to do, because when the fact that he had a kid came up and I said I had no interest in being seriously involved with a guy with a kid, although I was fine dating him casually, he freaked out about it. *Even though he'd spent a good twenty minutes talking about women wanting to be too serious.*

So, stay away from the ex talk. It just muddies the waters. Focus on this woman and what you want from her and don't get derailed by talking about other relationships and what you wanted from them. At least not until you hit that "share your soul" point in the relationship.

Don't Share Too Much

That leads me to add another one. I don't think this is so much a first date issue as a general early relationship issue, but it's worth keeping in mind.

I happen to be a very good listener who will encourage people to talk about whatever it is that's bothering them. I also give good advice and sympathy and support when this happens which makes people comfortable sharing with me things they don't often share with others.

Because of this, I run into a situation that's very challenging, which is that men who don't know me well enough to do so will talk to me about things they never talk to anyone about. Like a brother who was committed to a mental asylum or an ex-girlfriend who was so anorexic she had to be hospitalized or any of a number of other sensitive, personal topics. Things you shouldn't just share if that's not the type of person you are. And especially if the other person isn't being equally candid.

(And who knows maybe I am and don't see it that way because certain life events are so core to who I am that they come up whether someone else would consider that a serious revelation or not.)

While it can feel good to have that conversation, it can create an imbalance of intimacy in the relationship. You feel like you've bared your soul to this person, but they don't know that. For you, this was a huge emotionally weighted event to share this kind of thing. To them it was an emotional conversation that had depth to it, but not something they know they need to protect and handle with care. Not knowing you well enough, they assume that you are always this open which could lead to them mentioning it in a setting or context that feels hurtful to you.

So if you're sharing things that matter to you, make sure the other person is, too. Otherwise, hold back some at that early stage. Yes, true, someone has to go first at opening up, but do it a little bit at a time so you're both moving at the same pace and one of you doesn't get too far ahead of the other.

This section may not have made sense to some of you, and if it didn't, don't worry about it. But hopefully for those who've had this happen, it helped put it in context. As the person on the receiving end of these types of disclosures, let me assure you that any harm that was caused was not caused intentionally.

Don't Be Overly Creepy

By this I mean don't be overly sexual. Just like the emotional intimacy thing where you each need to take small steps towards the other, be sure she's on board with your level of sexual attention.

And it isn't enough that she not react negatively. You need her to be there with you, taking that next step.

What am I talking about?

Example time (again): I was on a first date with a guy who decided towards the end of the night that he should read my palm. It was basically a thinly-veiled excuse to hold my hand and gently stroke my palm with his finger.

Did I yank my hand away from his and tell him to go to hell?

No. I let him do it.

But I also didn't say, "My turn now" and do the same to him. Or let my hand linger in his. Or in any way cross that physical space between us or try to deepen the intimacy of the moment. He did his little hand-holding thing and then I took my hand out of his and drank some beer.

That was not the moment for him to step things up sexually. (But he tried anyway.)

So. How does this work?

You tell an off-color joke and then you see if she responds with one of her own. If she doesn't, you back off.

You let your arm or leg touch hers and you see if she keeps the contact or moves away or maybe even moves closer. If not, you back off.

You bring up some sex-related topic and you see if she just listens to you and changes the subject, or if she adds her own story or comment. If she doesn't add to the conversation, you retreat to something more neutral.

You try, you fail, you retreat.

You try, she matches you, you continue.

Some women will be right there with you. Some will not.

And don't think that because she isn't there in that moment that she isn't interested. She might have some rules about first dates. Or she might have something she needs to work through when it comes to you before she can be comfortable with that. (Like how in love you still are with your ex. Or how much of an ex she actually is.)

You need to give her space to come around, though. Push too hard and you're not getting that chance.

(And, by the way, it's okay for you to decide that you'd rather date the kind of woman who is right there with you from day one. If you think this woman is standoffish or prude or rude or whatever, you don't have to ask her out again. *Even if she's attractive.* I assume the reason you care about her looks is because you want something to happen with her? But if she's not really on the same page with you when it comes to that, it's probably not going to go well when it does happen.)

Leave Your Phone Alone

Let's drop back to a basic one. If you're on a date with a woman, be focused on her. That means no pausing every ten seconds to respond to texts and no taking phone calls unless they're unexpected ones you think might be important.

(I once got a call from my grandma in the middle of a date to tell me my mom was in the hospital. I didn't take the actual call, but did check the message since my grandma normally doesn't leave them.)

And stay off the internet, too. If your date goes to the bathroom, fine. Entertain yourself. But if she's sitting right there in front of you? Focus on her.

And expect her to do the same for you.

(Or I guess you could both be on your phones the whole time in which case you're well-matched, but ugh.

Who wants that? What kind of a relationship is it where you're both more interested in other events and people than spending time with one another?)

Don't Flirt With Others

This should be obvious, but don't hit on other women while you're on a date with this one.

You think it doesn't happen, but it does. When I was young and foolish I dated a guy who was every sort of wrong for me. And he really was the world's biggest, most ridiculous flirt. Got us free food at McDonald's one time, but it was completely inappropriate and I never put up with that shit from a guy again.

If you want to be a charming, flirtatious guy that every woman loves, be one. Just do it when you're alone. Not with your date sitting right there.

Now, some guys are just charming. It's like it oozes from their pores. That's fine. Although you'd be better off turning that charm on your date.

But asking some other woman if she has a boyfriend or telling her she's attractive or asking when she gets off or what her number is? No. That's too much.

Don't Insult Her

We touched on this a bit when I mentioned that arguing with a potential date isn't going to help get you to the actual date, but there's another one in here to consider, which is that it's never a good idea to criticize or insult your date.

When I told a friend of mine that I was writing this book and asked her for some of her horror stories—and she has a lot because she was much more open-minded about meeting up with her potential matches than I ever was—the first guy she thought of was the one who said, "You must've been hungry" when she finished eating her dinner.

Never comment on what a woman eats, whether it's too much or too little.

Our society has too many issues with women and food and weight, and a seemingly innocuous comment can actually be loaded with all sorts of judgmental bullshit most women aren't going to want to hear.

You want to ask if her food tastes good? Okay. You want a bite? Fine. You want to offer her a bite of yours? Fine. But don't comment on the type or quantity she just ate or didn't eat. Ever.

(There's a school of thought that some men follow that argues that insulting a woman is a good way to get her attention. It's included in a whole slew of dating books about unlocking the secrets to women and how to get any woman. My thoughts? Don't do it. Because for every woman that sort of thing works on, there's another who will never give you the time of day again. And, honestly, most men don't know the difference between being insulting and busting someone's chops a bit. You insult a woman, you're done. You playfully poke at her ego, you might be fine. But can you really tell the difference? Probably not. So best to not risk falling on the wrong side of that line.)

Compliment Her But Not Too Much

Should you compliment your date? Yeah, sure. It can help. A simple, "You look lovely this evening," never goes wrong.

Just be careful that your compliments don't turn to gushing. Remember that whole, you're her equal and you need to act it thing? Keep that in mind.

I've had guys go overboard on the compliments. Like they couldn't stop once they started. I've also had them compliment me but in a "oh, I didn't realize you were that far out of my league" sort of way.

(Typing that makes me sound so damned arrogant. But it really has happened. Like they knew I was smart, but they didn't realize I was that smart.)

So, anyway. One sincere, honest compliment and then you're done for the night.

Of course, as with all of my advice, take into account what type of woman this is and what she's indicated she likes or wants from men. I clearly don't like being put on a pedestal, but some women will eat that shit up. You need to know which you're dealing with and act accordingly.

SIDE NOTE:
WOMEN ARE INDIVIDUALS

I've mentioned this a few times, but let's go over it again. Because it really is central to you being successful at dating.

Women are individuals.

What works for one may not work for another.

You're probably thinking, well, duh. Of course women are individuals, aren't we all?

But when you're reading a book on how to approach a large group of people, be it women or co-workers or the general public, this can tend to get lost. And what ends up happening is you get told that X approach works all the time.

But, honestly, that's not true. I for one do not like getting flowers. And yet if you watch commercials in February of every year you'd walk away convinced that the way to show affection or interest to a woman is to give her a bunch of red roses. Or chocolate. Or a stuffed animal.

(For the record, two of the best gifts guys ever gave me were stuffed animals. But not just any stuffed animal.

In both cases the guy gave me a stuffed animal customized to me in some special way. One was an inside joke, one matched the colors of my apartment perfectly.)

Now, giving flowers can be a sort of cultural shortcut. We all know that red roses mean romantic interest so if you give them you're telling her that you are romantically interested.

But it's so generic. And there's no acknowledgement there that the woman is an individual who needs to be treated as unique.

You're far better off thinking about the specific woman you're dealing with and actually interacting with her on an individual basis.

Basically: Listen to what she says and respond to that. Don't base your actions or decisions on what you think women as a whole want or will do.

Like this book. I just told you all sorts of things not to do on a first date. And yet, if you talk to a bunch of happy couples you'll find that they violated one or more of these.

Maybe they slept with the person on the first date. Or stayed up until four in the morning talking about everything in their lives, including all of their exes and every deep intimate secret they'd never told anyone else.

Or maybe she was three hours late but he waited for her and it's now their favorite little story to tell.

So, while you should keep in mind these "rules", feel free to call an audible if it makes sense in the moment.

(Although, if you're really bad at reading women's cues, I'd suggest you don't actually try that. At least follow these rules until you're at date three or four.)

IT'S OKAY TO NOT WANT TO
GO OUT AGAIN

If you've been single long enough you've probably been told (at least I and most of my female friends have) that you should give someone a try. Go out on a few dates before you write them off. Don't be so picky.

Or, maybe this is more the scenario for men, you meet a woman who is so attractive that you can't think about anything else. Including the fact that she's awful for you.

So you keep going on dates with her even though it makes you miserable. Maybe you think once you sleep together it'll get better. (It won't. You'll just stay with her that much longer because, hey, sex.)

Don't do that to yourself. It's okay to go on one date and decide this person isn't the one for you.

And I'm not saying that just because I'm an insanely picky judgmental person who rarely changes my mind and has yet to give someone a second chance and be glad I did.

Most of my friends who are happily married or in good relationships felt a click with their significant other the first time they met them. They may not have dated them right away, because the person was in a relationship or a co-worker or whatever, but they did feel that little spark of interest.

It wasn't just physical attraction either. It was something more.

So if you're on a date and you don't feel anything positive about seeing this person again, move on. Because every moment you spend with this person who isn't right for you is a moment that you aren't spending on finding the right person for you.

I think too often people get scared or worried that they'll be alone and they settle for "good enough." But it isn't. That person you're settling for is someone else's dream partner. So let them go find that person who will adore them, and you find that person you'll adore and who'll adore you.

THE THIRD DATE ISSUE

While we're talking, let me tell you about the third date issue I see with too too many men.

On a first date I'm generally vetting a guy to see if we're compatible. So I'm listening to how he approaches the world and looking for any red flags that we won't work long-term. How does he talk about other people? Does he like his life? If not, is he doing anything to change it? Is he smart? Is he nice? Is he funny?

Basically, do I like this guy?

Unfortunately, most men aren't really listening to a thing I say.

I could tell them I engage in voodoo and cut the heads off chickens and they'd just shrug and smile and keep going. I call it the third-date problem. Because I swear that until we get past the third date the only thing on a guy's mind is whether he thinks he can sleep with me or not.

Only after we get past that point does he suddenly seem to realize that we have all sorts of differences that aren't going to work for him.

Now, granted, this is a broad generalization and not all men are that way. But you'd be surprised how many first dates I've been on where it was abundantly clear to me that we were not compatible at all and the guy didn't seem to notice.

I've even pointed these things out to some of the guys. Like, "Hey, you are devoutly religious and want to raise your children in your faith and I am not willing to do that." And they say something like, "Oh, you'll come around." Or "Oh, we'll work through it."

No we won't.

But because the guy is so caught up on the physical side of things he doesn't see the rest of it.

That puts all of the heavy lifting of judging the relationship's potential on me. And, yes, there are people who will happily sleep with someone they don't necessarily like and be fine with it, but I'm not that person. So it's a waste of a guy's time to ignore the non-physical for the physical.

So all I'm saying is maybe try to step back a bit and focus less on how attractive your date is and more on whether the two of you could stand to be stuck in an elevator together for four hours straight.

If you couldn't, then walk away.

Looks are not everything.

I know, sacrilege. But seriously? If you're in this for the long-term, remember that people get old. They get wrinkles and cellulite and serious illnesses and things that you don't want sagging start to sag. Badly. If you want a relationship that will last the rest of your life, you need to like this person enough and they need to like you enough that none of that matters.

Think about it.

But I digress.

WRAPPING UP THE FIRST DATE

So you had a first date. It went well. Time for it to end. What do you do so you can see this woman again?

If it was a really fabulous date, you don't have to do much. Because you probably already geeked out together over something you both like and you already have a specific thing you want to do together. Like, "Oh my god, I've been dying to go to that new sushi place, too," sort of thing.

In that case, when it comes time to wrap things up, you say, "So what do you think? You want to go to that sushi place on Thursday?"

And she says, "Absolutely." Or, "Oh, I have plans on Thursday, but what about Sunday?"

And you make a *specific* plan to get together to do a *specific* thing at a *specific* time.

If you didn't have that fabulous a date, that doesn't mean all hope is lost. You can still do the standard, "I had a good time. You want to get together again?" and she will say, "Sure, I'd like that." And then you will call her and set something up later.

But keep this in mind—especially if it was a never-met-before date—until you have firm plans set, you really don't know if you're going to get a second date or not.

We're back into the "yeah, sure" stage of things. The "it's easier for me to say yes than to reject him to his face" stage.

And if you press to make firm plans and she's not quite sure she wants to really see you again, she's gonna sidestep that question and say something like, "I really can't commit to anything right now. Work's gonna be insane this week and I need to see what my boss is going to throw at me before I know if I'll have any free time."

She likely won't tell you right there to your face that she doesn't want to see you again.

So how can you tell if you've got a shot?

Well, do you have her phone number? Or email?

Or are you still relying on the dating site you used to meet her?

If you end the first date without getting direct contact information for this woman, no matter how well it feels like it went, chances are you're not going to see her again.

Because all she has to do is say, "yeah, sure," and then go home and close down the match. So, if you can, be sure to ask for her number or email if you don't already have it. If she hesitates to give it to you at this stage, you're very likely not going to see her again.

But she won't tell you that, she'll just tell you to reach out through the site because it's easier that way.

WHAT YOU SHOULD NEVER DO:
A CASE STUDY

I've definitely had guys I would've probably gone out with again who dropped the ball in one way or another and never tried again. Like the guy who was a friend of a friend and asked about going out but didn't get my number and made no effort to follow up with our mutual friend.

There was another guy who I'd met online dating who said he'd reach out to me and didn't and I think it was because he got home and thought it was my turn to message him on the site and didn't realize he could message me, and I wasn't quite interested enough to reach out to him. (Of course, maybe he got home and thought "eh, not interested" but I'm a pretty good judge of a guy's interest and I think he was interested enough that that's not what happened.)

So, to a certain extent, I would encourage guys to try a little extra after a first date if they really like a woman and haven't been told "no" directly.

(Although, know that in most instances you're wasting your time pursuing her further.)

(And if she is the type of woman who *deliberately* tries to make it hard for you so she can know you're really interested, think about whether that's what you want in your life. No matter how attractive a woman is, she should treat you with decency.)

What you should not do, under any circumstances, is what this guy did to my friend.

A bit of background: They went on two dates. She probably should've called it after one date, but my friend is nice and was very serious about meeting someone so she went on date number two. Just in case. After that second date she told him straight up in an email that she wasn't interested in seeing him again.

What did he do next?

He called her.

When she didn't take his call, he sent her an email acknowledging that his continued pursuit of her might be pushing her even further away or seen as desperate. He then proceeded to write a number of lengthy paragraphs about why *he* liked *her* so much.

When that didn't work he showed up at her office with flowers.

No.

No.

No.

Do not do this. For every one woman that is won over by your ardent interest and inability to give up on her, there will be eight that send your heartfelt email to their friends with an "OMG" comment, and one who calls the cops to see if she can get a restraining order. (I suspect you know by now which one I would be.)

What is so wrong with what this guy did?

First, never, ever show up at a woman's work after she's rejected you. You may think it makes perfect sense because you know she'll be there and all you want to do is talk and you know you can find her there.

She thinks (or maybe this is just me) about all those crazy stalker types who've killed their ex-wives or ex-girlfriends by showing up at their work brandishing a weapon and demanding that she talk to them.

(As I write this, the news coverage has a story about a man who did this at an elementary school and ended up killing his wife, himself, and an eight-year-old child. No matter what week I chose to write this, there would be a story like that on the news. Yes, women can do this crazy shit, too. And women have killed their partners. But it is far more likely that a man will kill his partner.)

So some guy a woman rejected showing up at her work unasked for is a HUGE red flag. HUGE.

DO NOT DO THIS. EVER.

EVER. EVER. EVER.

She said no. Move on.

But if you can't bring yourself to let go of this perfect woman that easily, then you need to make your case from a distance and you need to focus on what she overlooked about you.

You do not write to her to tell her how beautiful she is and how much *you* want *her*. She knows that. Chances are, if she's decent looking, this is not the first time in her life that a man found her attractive but she wasn't interested in him. Your interest in her is irrelevant.

You need *her* to be interested in *you*.

So if you want to win her over, you need to tell her what it is about you that you somehow failed to convey in the dates you went on that she would want.

Or you clarify the misunderstanding you guys had that led to her deciding she didn't want to see you again. (For example, "I'm sorry about that scene at the restaurant.

That was my sister playing a joke on me, but you didn't stick around long enough for her to tell you that.")

Often in these cases a man keeps reaching out because he wants the woman and he thinks for some reason the degree to which he wants her should convince her to want him back.

That's not how it works.

(And if you are someone who thinks like that? If you've done something like this in the past? Been so in love with a woman that you couldn't let go or see why she didn't want you back? You need to sit down with a professional to work through why you did it and how not to do it again.)

HOW TO OVERCOME AN INITIAL REJECTION

So what *do* you do if you really liked a woman and she told you straight-up that she's not interested in seeing you again. Or if she ghosted you or shut down your online match after the date?

My personal recommendation is to move on. Chalk it up to not everyone is compatible and what you think you see or feel is not what the other person is seeing or feeling.

Nine times out of ten she knows her own mind and you trying to convince her to give you another chance isn't going to work. It'll just be awkward for both of you.

If she shut down the match or told you no—so took a direct action to not see you again—the chances of bringing her around are about one in a hundred. If that.

But sometimes things do fall through the cracks.

I had a guy email me a while back and his email ended up in my spam filter. I did see it, but many women wouldn't have. And he'd be sitting there thinking, "Oh, she doesn't want to see me," when what really happened is she never even knew he reached out.

So, this is what you can do if you really must:

If you called her and left a message and didn't get a response, you can send her a quick email that says, "Hey, tried to call you. Don't know if you got the message. Call or write back at XXX-XXXX. I'd love to see you again."

If you emailed her and got no response, you can drop her a quick text. "Sent you an email. Was hoping to get together again. Reach out if you're interested."

Something like that. It's short and to the point and the assumption here is that she didn't get your first communication. It's the only reason you should be reaching out to her—if you think she somehow didn't get that first message.

What do you do if you only have one way of reaching her? A way that clearly didn't work the first time around.

You can see if there's an easy second way to reach her. Say you have mutual friends on Facebook. You could reach out to her that way. But even as I type this I'm thinking "no, no, no." Same with LinkedIn or Twitter or finding her business email.

It's all just…too stalkery.

Now, full disclosure here. I have in the past (a) dropped by the work of a guy who casually said we should go out some time to ask him when that was going to happen and (b) messaged some guy I'd met and liked after tracking him down on Facebook.

In both cases I was "successful" at reviving something that I had no other way to move forward because I didn't have their phone numbers or emails. (In hindsight, both were a bad idea. But it did work. And we did go out or stay in touch after I did it.)

But, I'm a woman. And the rules, like it or not, are different for women.

Or, and this is even worse, the rules are different for

someone you find attractive.

If I sat next to some really good-looking guy on a plane flight and we had a great conversation but then didn't exchange numbers and he tracked me down via my LinkedIn, I'd probably be more flattered than disturbed.

But if I had a lengthy conversation with some guy on a plane flight who wasn't attractive to me and he did the same thing, I'd probably be a little creeped out.

And in this case, we're talking about a situation where you already had a date. You had your chance to reel her in and you blew it somehow.

So, really? Best to move on. Your level of interest likely does not match hers.

Plenty of fish in the sea. If it was meant to be you'll cross paths again. Yada, yada, yada.

AFTER THE FIRST DATE:
KEEP PLAYING IT COOL

So what about if you did ask her out for a second date and she said yes. Now what?

Now we move into the "everyone is different" stage of dating. Where how you act and behave is dictated by the person you're dating.

Seriously, after that first date, it's all about the two individuals and how they move forward together. But I will tell you that I've had a good first date with a guy and then decided I really didn't want to see him again because of how he acted before the second date.

I already mentioned one of the examples above where the guy called brunch "bunch" and then argued with me about what it was.

Another was a guy who became way too serious way too fast. I honestly think wedding bells were going off in his head after that first date. He started sending me virtual roses and being far too aggressive about how much he liked me.

Some women will eat that up. The more the better. And maybe if he'd been a different guy, I would've eaten it up, too. But I wasn't as interested as he was, so all it did was scare me off.

So, after the first date, no matter how you're feeling and even if she said yes to another one and is responding to your messages, pay attention to how often she responds and what she says.

Does she take your phone calls or just text or email or message? If so, how long do you guys stay on the phone when you talk? Is she flirty? Is she all business? If you send a text, does she respond right away? Or wait for a day?

Whatever she does, mirror her. If she's all about the details of the second date and not interested in talking or communicating back and forth, then be that way, too. Don't send five messages for every one she sends you.

(And again, as a woman, I can think of situations where I did these things I'm telling you not to do and it worked, but...don't do it. It never ends well. You want a balance with this other person so you're moving forward at the same pace. It's too easy to get too far ahead of them and then have it fall apart, or find that you feel very different things from what they feel.)

But it's also okay to move fast *as long as she is, too.*

My friend who is happily married and expecting her first child moved in with her now-husband within a couple of weeks of their first date. And they were married eight months later. So things can move fast. But both people have to be on board with it. You can't just really like someone and make it happen on your own. That's a good way to lose them instead.

JUST FOR KICKS: MY REASONS FOR NOT WANTING TO SEE A GUY AGAIN

This is not a list you should use as any sort of resource. This is more a list that shows that sometimes it's not about you. Or it is about you but not in any way you can fix. Some matches just don't work and that's part of dating and something you need to understand so you can move forward and find the woman who is right for you.

Also, note that some of these were for the same person, so in isolation they weren't a reason to reject a guy but when combined with a few others they were.

Ready? Reasons I didn't want to go out with a guy again:

1. He liked cats and had one at home. (I'm allergic and hate them.)

2. He had a long-term illness that was going to impact his quality of life. (Been there, done that, didn't want to do it again.)

3. He showed signs of anger issues. (I have zero tolerance for men with tempers.)

4. At first I thought he was a gracious loser and then I realized he was just really used to losing at things. (As someone who is fiercely competitive, this was a turn off.)

5. He was overly aggressive sexually and not attractive enough to me for that to work.

6. He had a kid.

7. He had no ambition.

8. We talked about accounting for the entire date. (I can talk about anything with anyone for an hour, but that doesn't mean I want to repeat that experience ever again.)

9. He called himself a foodie but we went to a chain Italian restaurant for the date.

10. He wanted to split the check. (This only comes into play when combined with others on the list.)

11. He was incredibly awkward to talk to. There was no flow to our conversation.

12. It felt more like a job interview than a date. He asked rapid-fire questions about where I wanted to be in five years.

13. He wanted marriage and kids NOW.

14. He seemed a bit intimidated by what he learned about me and I'd been holding back a number of things.

15. We had absolutely nothing in common.

16. I didn't find him attractive. (Looks are only part of this for me. A really interesting personality can partially compensate for not being classically good-looking.)

17. He talked down about others a lot.

18. He was too focused on status and one-upping others.

19. Our attitudes towards money were not compatible.

20. Our backgrounds were too different for me to ever be comfortable with him.

21. He was too nice. (I knew the first time I was in a bad mood I'd tear him to shreds.)

22. He referred to women who wear a size large at Victoria's Secret as fat. (Even while eyeing me up and down like some prize piece of meat.)

23. He was too focused on his career or hobbies or other interests to actually have room for me in his life.

24. He told me stories that showed he would cut corners or break rules at work or in his career if it let him get ahead temporarily.

25. He wasn't smart.

26. He was offensive.

27. He said he hated living in my home state and wanted to leave as soon as possible.

28. He wasn't close to his family.

29. He didn't like dogs.

30. He was very religious.

31. He was very anti-religion.

32. He clearly wasn't interested in a committed relationship.

33. His appearance was sloppy.

34. He had a go-nowhere job and no apparent ambition.

35. He had failed at things I thought should be easy. In other words, I didn't respect him.

CONCLUSION

So there you have it. Let's see if we can sum up.

- Until you actually make it to the first date, you aren't guaranteed that that date will happen.

- Especially if you met the woman in person, she may not have had any intent of ever seeing you again.

- Even if she did think she wanted to meet up with you, you can turn that yes into a no by saying something rude or getting too comfortable too soon or making her realize she's out of your league or failing to manage the negotiation of where to go and what to do effectively.

- The first date can also be fraught with opportunities to blow things and lose the girl.

- You want to be on time, pay for her drink or meal without making a big deal out of it, dress nicely, and focus on her.

- On a date you shouldn't be rude to other people, talk about your ex, overshare, get too sexual if she isn't onboard with it, flirt with others, insult her, or spend too much time on your phone.

- All of this goes out the window depending on the woman you're dealing with and your best bet to dating success is to pay attention to her and what she wants.

- You should have some pride in yourself and insist that a woman treat you right as well.

- Even if a woman is attractive, that doesn't mean you need to put up with poor treatment. Instead, move on to find a woman who will treat you well.

- Men can sometimes get a little too hung up on the physical side of things early on and you'd be much better off if you stepped back and made sure there was actually something there between you other than your physical attraction to her.

- If a woman does turn you down, best to just move on.

- If you can't bring yourself to move on, then try one simple, basic attempt to show her why you are worth giving another chance (and it can't be because you really like her), and then move on.

- Under no circumstance should you ever show up at the workplace of a woman who rejected you.

- There are any number of reasons a woman might not want to see you again that have nothing to do with you and everything to do with her, so don't get hung up on it. Just move on to someone who will like you for who you are.

Bottom line is to try to make the best impression you can until you're about three dates in or she's so obviously infatuated with you that you're on the right track. But accept that not all dates will work out either and move on from those that don't so you can focus on the ones that will. And applying the golden rule of treating others how you'd like to be treated is going to overcome many of the reasons a first date doesn't succeed.

I know the whole process can be a frustrating nightmare. But I also have any number of friends who've persevered and found someone who truly made their lives better, so don't give up. Remember what you want out of a relationship and insist on getting that. Don't settle because you're tired or desperate. It'll happen. You just have to push through.

Good luck!

ABOUT THE AUTHOR

Cassie Leigh likes to write about what she knows, which it would seem are the pains of dating, cooking for one, and raising a puppy.

* * *

You can reach the author at
cassieleighauthor@gmail.com.

www.ingramcontent.com/pod-product-compliance
Lightning Source LLC
Chambersburg PA
CBHW071239020426
42333CB00015B/1541